Drama Games
for Kids

111 Theatre Activities to
Energize Your Drama Class

A BEAT BY BEAT BOOK

ISBN: 069266436X
ISBN-13: 978-0692664360

CONTENTS

IMPROV   98

WARM-UPS

Introductions & Applause

Purpose: To help kids introduce themselves and to raise the comfort level of the group. Encourages kids to overcome any stage fright.

Procedure:

1. Using either a real door or an imaginary door (which you create for the players), each player must come up one by one, walk through the door to "enter" the stage and introduce themselves. Each player says "Hi, my name is _____" and says one interesting thing about themselves. You can have them add more to the speech, but try not to make it long or complicated. The point is to make this an easy task.
2. After each introduction, the audience must enthusiastically applaud as the player stays up on stage and takes it all in.

Note: Do *no* coaching here. The point is to let each player perform their introduction, without criticism whatsoever. The only thing you *can* coach them on is waiting for the applause. Don't let them run off the stage before they take it in!

Bippity Bippity Bop

Purpose: To increase focus, attentiveness and work on quick decision making. Raises comfort level of a group and releases energy.

Procedure:

The entire group stands in a circle and the teacher stands in the middle of the circle.

<u>Level 1:</u> The teacher points at a player in the circle and says as fast as she can the words "bippity bippity bop". The player chosen must say "bop" before the teacher reaches the end of the phrase. If the teacher points to a player and says only "bop", the player chosen must stay quiet and not say a word. The objective for the teacher in the first scenario is to beat players from saying "bop" in time and in the second scenario to get players to mistakenly say "bop". Continue for several rounds.

<u>Level 2:</u> After the group gets the hang of Level 1, it is time to add another dimension. If the teacher points to a player and says "haunted house" the player must crouch down and in a ghoulish voice say "Come in! Come in!". The two students on the player's left and right must use both their arms to make the roof of a house over the player that is crouched.

<u>Level 3:</u> If the teacher points to a player and says "Hawaii", the chosen player must do the hula while the players on the left and right puts their hands and arms up like palm trees.

<u>Level 4:</u> If the teacher points to a player and says "Godzilla", the chosen player must stomp in place and roar as if he was Godzilla while the players on the left and right cower and scream.

If you have time, as a class make up more rules and actions.

Once the class gets the hang of it, you can add an elimination mode where if a player makes a mistake or doesn't respond in time, he/she must sit down. Continue until you have a winner.

Zip, Zap, Zop!

Purpose: To increase focus, attentiveness and work on quick decision making. Raises comfort level of a group and releases energy.

Procedure:

Level 1: Players stand in a circle. Player A claps his hands, ending in a pointing position toward the direction of another player. Simultaneously Player A will say the nonsense word "Zip!" Player B repeats the clap and action while saying "Zap!" at another player. Player C repeats the clap action while saying "Zop!" at yet another player.

Players can clap and point at any player they choose, but they must follow the pattern "Zip, Zap, Zop."

This game is typically played as an elimination game where everyone who says a word out of order (ie. saying "Zop" instead of "Zip") or takes too long is eliminated from the game till there is only one player left.

Level 2: After the group gets the hang of Level 1, you can have them remove either the clap action or saying the words "Zip, Zap, Zop." Focus is passed from one player to another by using just the word pattern or by clap action only, not both.

Level 3: When they've mastered Level 2, remove the clap action as well as saying any words. Focus is passed by making direct eye contact only.

Name Game

Purpose: To learn names and something about each player. To understand how to pantomime and communicate ideas.

Procedure:

1. Gather players in a circle.
2. Have each player say their first name and pantomime a gesture for each syllable in their name. The action should be simple and can demonstrate a hobby, interest, or something that they do everyday. Example: I say "Pam-e-la" and gesture a paddle stroke on each side of my body (one stroke per syllable, on my left-right-left side) to show I like to canoe.
3. Each player individually says their name while demonstrating the gesture then all together the group repeats the name and gesture.
4. Repeat the process around the circle so everyone shares their name and gesture.
5. Let any player up for the challenge demonstrate the name and gesture of every person in the group. This can be done in the same session if time allows or at a later session.

Lap, Lap, Clap, Snap!

Purpose: To practice learning everyone's names and rhythm coordination. Raises the comfort level of the group.

Procedure:

1. Sit on the floor in a big group circle.
2. Have everyone go around and introduce their first name.
3. Teach the group the vocal and movement pattern "Lap, Lap, Clap, Snap". This is done by patting your lap with both hands twice in a row, clapping your hands in front of you, and then snapping your fingers with both hands. Do it several times as a group until everyone in the circle is comfortable with the rhythm.
4. Then the game begins. The leader starts the pattern: "Lap, Lap, Clap, Snap." But instead of saying "Snap", the leader calls out the name of a player in the circle.
5. That player whose name was called out must then continue the pattern, calling out a different player's name in the place of the "Snap".

For example:
LEADER: Lap, Lap, Clap Sasha!
SASHA: Lap, Lap, Clap, John!
JOHN: Lap, Lap, Clap, Linda!
etc.

6. The trick is to never break the rhythm. This will probably take some practice rounds at first. Practice until everyone is comfortable with the pattern.
7. After awhile, consider adding an elimination mode. Where any time the rhythm is broken, the person who broke the rhythm is out. The player sitting next to the eliminated player should start the rhythm again.
8. When everyone gets the hang of the game, increase the fun by speeding up the rhythm!

Whoosh!

Purpose: To increase focus, attentiveness and work on quick decision making. Raises the comfort level of a group while releasing energy.

Procedure:

1. Everybody stands in a circle.
2. Start with one player, who gestures a throwing motion with both hands out towards her neighbor while saying "Whoosh".
3. That next player passes the "Whoosh" to his neighbor. This continues until the "Whoosh" is passed around the entire circle.
4. There are four other sounds/movements that can be used: Whoa!, Zap, Grooooooovelicious, Freakout.
5. **Whoa!** – The player holds up both hands in a stop motion. A "Whoa" changes the direction of the "Whoosh". The "Whoosh" player must pass it to the neighbor in the opposite direction.
6. **Zap** – Instead of passing the "Whoosh" to your neighbor, a "Zap" is passed to any player you pick. Clap your hands one time with both hands together, ending with fingers pointed away from your body towards the direction of another player. The receiving player continues next with either a "Whoosh" to his neighbor or can "Zap" to another player. A "Whoa" after a "Zap" returns the play back to the zapper.
7. **Grooooooovelicious** – The player moves her body down and up in a *groovy* way. Then the entire group repeats the action while saying, "Grooooooovelicious". Afterwards, the player who called out "Grooooooovelicious" sets the "Whoosh" back in motion to her neighbor in either direction.
8. **Freakout** – The player waves both hands in the air while saying "Freakout!". Everybody screams and moves to the center and after freaking out forms a new circle. The player who called out "Freakout" sets the "Whoosh" back in motion.

Variations:
1. You can invent other sounds and gestures.
2. Begin an elimination mode in which players that make a mistake must sit down, until there's only two players left standing.

Splat!

Purpose: To warm up the body and voice. Encourages focus and quick decision making raising attentiveness.

Procedure:

1. The group stands forming a circle with the teacher in the middle.
2. The teacher throws an imaginary pie at one player in the circle.
3. That chosen player must duck and the two players on either side of him throws an imaginary pie at one other and shouts "SPLAT!".
4. If the chosen player doesn't duck, he is out. If he does duck in time, the last player to throw their pie on either side of him is out.
5. Continue until you are down to just two players left.
6. When there are only two players left begin THE DUEL. The two remaining players stand back to back in the middle of the circle. Pick a category of objects to call out, such as *cereal*. Each time the teacher calls out a type of cereal, the two players take one step forward. When a word that is NOT a type of cereal is called out, they must throw their pies. The first to throw the pie at the correct time is the winner!

Bomb and Shield

Purpose: A useful warm-up or a mid-session activity if kids have been sitting for a while. Encourages attentiveness and responses.

Procedure:

1. The group stands forming a circle.
2. Each player silently picks two players from the circle and labels one as the "bomb" and the other their "shield". This is decided silently in their heads.
3. When you say "Go" all the players must move around the room always keeping their "shield" between themselves and the "bomb". They must never stop moving.
4. After awhile, say "Switch!". Now the "bomb" player becomes your "shield" and your "shield" player becomes the "bomb".
5. At the end of the activity have the group form a circle and each reveal who was their bomb and who was their shield.

Pass the Sound

Purpose: To warm up the body and voice. To increase focus and raise attentiveness.

Procedure:

1. In a standing circle, pass a "Whoosh" around the circle. This is done by saying "Whoosh!" and gesturing with both hands a throwing motion toward the person next to you.
2. After it goes around a couple times stop the "Whoosh!" and send a "Bing!" going the opposite way of the circle, using a different hand gesture.
3. Now tell the players they need to put their focus caps on, because you're going to send a "Whoosh!" going one direction, then a "Bing!" going the opposite direction simultaneously.
4. At some point "Whoosh" and "Bing" will overlap over one player, so they need to be prepared.
5. Try this out a few rounds. If they're up for it, add in a third sound and gesture, "Ooga!".

Look and Scream

Purpose: To work on focus and raise attentiveness. Increases reaction and response senses.

Procedure:

1. The group stands forming a circle.
2. Tell everyone to look down toward the ground.
3. Assign one player to be the counter. The counter is in charge of saying "1, 2, 3…Look!"
4. On "Look" everyone must look up directly at someone in the circle.
5. If the player you are looking at is not looking back at you, you are *safe*. And if the player you are looking at is looking back at you too, you both must scream "ahh!" and fall to the ground.
6. The counter begins another round with the remaining players standing in the circle.
7. Play until everyone is sitting or there's just one person remaining.

Keeper of the Keys

Purpose: To warm up bodies and increase focus. This is a simple game that is useful for very young actors (age 5-8).

Procedure:

1. One player, The Keeper, stands stage right with his back to the other players. A set of keys is placed at her feet.
2. All other players stand stage left, facing the *Keeper's* back.
3. When the Keeper says "Go", the group can move toward the Keeper to try and get the keys. When the Keeper turns around everyone must freeze. If the Keeper sees anyone *unfrozen* that player must go back to the start.
4. This continues until one player grabs the keys. This player now becomes the Keeper.

Notes:
Once the group gets the hang of the game, you can introduce variations that will help them explore different characters. (i.e. they must move and freeze as ballerinas, "tigers", "80-year olds", etc.)

Alien, Tiger, Cow

Purpose: To raise the comfort level of the group. Encourages kids to make choices while warming up voices and bodies.

Procedure:

1. The group stands forming a circle.
2. On the count of "3", the players have the choice of being one of three things (i.e. rock, paper or scissors: Alien, Tiger or Cow:

   ALIEN – players hold their fingers up to their head like   antennae and say "Bleep, bleep, bleep"

   TIGER – players throw their hands out like claws and say "Roooar!"

   COW – players put their hands on their tummies with fingers sticking out like utters and say "Mooo"

3. On the count of "3" everyone has the choice of being one of these things.
4. Whichever one of these things is the minority of the group, those players must leave the circle. (If there are 4 Aliens, 7 Tigers, and 3 Cows, the Cows are the minority and must leave the circle.)
5. Continue until there are only 1 or 2 players left.

Variation:

A different goal to playing this game is for everyone to become the SAME character (no elimination). Obviously it will take a few turns for this to happen. Let the players organically try to figure it out.

Greetings

Purpose: To break the ice with a new group. Encourages players to interact, make choices and explore characters.

Procedure:

1. Ask the players to walk around the room greeting each other.
2. First, allow them to greet each other however they feel comfortable (usually with a handshake or a wave).
3. Then, have the players greet each other in a specific way. Encourage them to continue walking around the room, greeting different people every time. Here are some options:
    - Greet someone you don't really trust.
    - Greet someone like they are a long lost friend.
    - Greet someone who has really bad breathe.
    - Greet someone like you have a crush on them.
    - Greet each other with a random, made-up language (gibberish). The person receiving the greeting should respond in the same fashion.
    - Greet someone like you are a cowboy.
    - Greet someone like you are a soldier.
    - Greet someone like you are a business person very late to a meeting.
    - Greet someone like an elderly person who desperately wants someone to talk to.
4. For older groups, you can continue this exercise by leading into an improvised two-person scene. Ask two players to take the stage, and assign them each one of the suggestions above. Have them begin with a greeting, then have them continue the scene until you say stop. (For example, Player A is an elderly person who wants someone to talk to, and Player B is a business person late to a meeting. Begin with a greeting, then continue the scene…action!)

Toilet Paper Icebreaker

Purpose: To break the ice with a new group. Encourages kids to share and practice speaking in front of a group.

Procedure:

1. The group sits forming a circle.
2. Hold up a roll of toilet paper. Tell the group to pass it around the circle, and each player can tear off as many or as few sheets as they wish.
3. After the roll has made it all the way around the circle, reveal the "twist" to the game. For every sheet that a player took, they have to share with the the group something about themselves.

EXAMPLE: If Isabel took five sheets, she says: 1) I like to dance. 2) My favorite color is purple. 3) I have a dog named Sammy. 4) This summer I went to Hawaii. 5) I'm really afraid of snakes.

4. Not only will the group learn from the information each student shares, but it will reveal the different personalities based on who took a lot of sheets and who took only a few.
5. Afterwards, have everyone toss their sheet into the center. Tell them that this pile represents all the new information we now know about each other.

Name Chant

Purpose: To practice rhythm coordination. To raise the comfort level of the group.

Procedure:

1. The group stands forming a circle.
2. Start the simple rhythm using both hands that alternates with a pat on the legs and then a clap: *Pat, Clap, Pat, Clap, etc.*
3. One player at a time says the chant below, while the rest of the group keeps the rhythm and says "Yeah!" after each line:

PLAYER:	GROUP:
My name is [name]	*Yeah!*
And I am [age]	*Yeah!*
I like to [action]	*Yeah!*
And it goes like this [gesture]	

After the last line, the player demonstrates the action. The group says:

> *[action] high!*
> *[action] low!*
> *[action] high!*
> *[action] low!*

The group does the gesture high and low respectively. So the full sequence might go something like this:

PLAYER:	GROUP:
My name is Linda	*Yeah!*
And I am ten	*Yeah!*
I like to swim	*Yeah!*
And it goes like this…	
(Linda demonstrates swimming)	

EVERYONE:
(Group gestures swimming.)
Swimming...high!
Swimming...low!
Swimming...high!
Swimming...low!

The patting and clapping rhythm resumes and it's the next player's turn. Continue until every player has had a turn.

Note:

The second line (about age) can be changed to anything you want the students to know more about each other. If you're rehearsing a play, the whole chant can be done as "your character" from the play. What type of activity does your character really enjoy?

Shake It Off

Purpose: To lift the energy of a group. *Not* recommend for focus or calming down a rowdy group. Helpful before a performance or loosening nerves.

Procedure:

1. The group stands forming a circle.
2. As a group, players must count down from 8 while shaking out each of their limbs. The order is right arm, left arm, right leg, left leg. Then they will count down from 7, then 6, etc. until they reach 1. They should increasingly get louder and louder throughout.

> ENTIRE GROUP
> Right arm: "8, 7, 6, 5, 4, 3, 2, 1!"
> Left arm: "8, 7, 6, 5, 4, 3, 2, 1!"
> Right leg: "8, 7, 6, 5, 4, 3, 2, 1!"
> Left leg: "8, 7, 6, 5, 4, 3, 2, 1!"
> Right arm: "7, 6, 5, 4, 3, 2, 1!"
> Left arm: "7, 6, 5, 4, 3, 2, 1!"
> Right leg: "7, 6, 5, 4, 3, 2, 1!"
> Left leg: "7, 6, 5, 4, 3, 2, 1!" …etc. until….
> Right arm: "1!"
> Left arm: "1!"
> Right leg: "1!"
> Left leg: "1!"

Notes:
1. Shake it off is often over used. If it's used in every single class it's a time-killer and doesn't encourage kids creatively. As I mentioned above, its just a useful way to loosen up and energize a group before a performance.
2. Consider playing Taylor Swift's "Shake it Off" during this activity and have them count in rhythm to the song.
3. For a super quick version of the game, have the group count down by even numbers until they get to 1. (8-6-4-2-1!)

Zombie Name Game

Purpose: To help kids (and the teacher) learn everyone's name. A active variation to the standard name game.

Procedure:

1. The group stands forming a circle.
2. Going around the circle, have each player loudly says his/her name as a zombie. ("Saaaarrraaaaahhhhh!")
3. Then choose one player to be the "zombie". The "zombie" walks in the middle of the circle zombie-style, with his arms stretched out front, head tilted to the side.
4. Call out a player's name. The zombie must walk toward that chosen player.
5. The chosen player must try to call out a different player's name before the zombie reaches him/her.
6. If the zombie is able to tag the player before he/she can callout a name, that tagged player now becomes the zombie.

Meet My Friend

Purpose: To increase listening and communication skills. A unique way to allow kids to get to know each other at the beginning session.

Procedure:

1. In your head, divide the number of players in the group by 2. (If there are 30 players in your group, dividing by 2 equals 15).
2. The group stands forming a circle. Starting from your left, have each player consecutively count up to 15. When you reach 15, the next player in the circle restarts at 1 and the rest of the circle counts up to 15 again.
3. Have each number find his/her pair (The 1s, the 2s, the 3s, etc.). You should have 15 pairs. (The goal of the first three steps is simply to randomize the pairs.)
4. Have each pair select an A and a B partner.
5. Instruct the players that you are going to set a timer and for one minute A must tell B as many things about himself as possible. (school, grade, favorite subject, favorite food, favorite music, etc.)
6. Start timer and let them go.
7. Then for one minute B must tell A as many things about herself as possible.
8. Start timer and let them go.
9. Call everyone back into a circle.
10. Going around the circle, each student must say three things about their partner beginning with this phrase "Meet my friend…".

For example: "Meet my friend Jenny, she is in 4th grade, she loves to play Minecraft, and she has really cool shoes."

Pro Tip: Consider, after letting one minute run out, announcing you're giving them an additional "30 more seconds and GO!" Sometimes this will force the kids to communicate greater information that goes beyond just the surface.

Drawing Introduction

Purpose: To make choices based on observations while raising the comfort level of a group. A unique way to allow kids to get to know each other at the beginning session.

Procedure:

1. Randomly divide the group into pairs.
2. Provide each player with a blank piece of paper and something to write with.
3. Instruct the players to silently think about items or objects in their lives that are important to them. For example, a player who loves sports might draw a football. Or perhaps there's a special family heirloom that has been passed down. Or maybe a musical instrument. The objects should reveal something specific about each individual.
4. Give the group 2-3 minutes to silently draw 5 of these objects on their piece of paper. If they can draw more items than that, great.
5. Remind the players that drawing ability doesn't matter at all, just to do the best they can.
6. After the drawings are complete, have each player take a turn at being the "Detective" and guess as much as they can about their partner based on the "evidence" (their drawing).
7. The partner should remain silent until the Detective is finished.
8. When the Detective is finished they can chat freely about what they got right or wrong during this "interview".
9. Bring the whole group together and ask each player to introduce their partner to the class and reveal out loud what they have discovered about them based on the drawing "evidence" and "interview".

ENSEMBLE BUILDING

Human Knot

Purpose: To creatively work as a group. Encourages team building and problem solving.

Procedure:

1. Group stands forming a circle. Have everyone come in really close toward the middle of the circle, with their hands stretched out in the center.
2. Everyone grabs two hands. Not the hands of the player standing next them and not both hands of the same player.
3. Tell the group they must untie the knot without anyone ever letting go of their hands.
4. Counsel them to go very slowly and be very gentle.
5. Do it once allowing the students to talk and once in silence.

One Word Story

Purpose: To creatively work as a group. Encourages team building and attentiveness.

Procedure:

1. Group sits forming a circle.
2. One player says a single word to begin a story.
3. The player to his left says another word, then the next player says another word, continuing around the circle.
4. The object is to tell a coherent story, one word at a time.

Note:

Consider coaching the group to include a conflict, or remind them to have a beginning, middle and end to their story as they go along.

Conducted Story

Purpose: To creatively work as a group. Encourages team building and attentiveness.

1. In a line facing the audience, players tell a group story.
2. One player is designated "the conductor" and kneels in front facing the line.
3. When "the conductor" points to someone they must begin to tell a story.
4. After a few beats have passed which allows the first player to develop a story line, the conductor randomly points at a different player who must pick up the story exactly where the first student left off. It can be mid-sentence or mid-word.
5. Continue until the story is completed.

Note:

Consider encouraging the first player to choose a distinct character trait when beginning the story. For example, as a grumpy old man, an excited teenager, etc. All other players must tell the story as this "character".

Walking Blind (Trust Exercise #1)

Purpose: To elevate the comfort level and trust among the group.

Procedure:

1. This is a silent activity.
2. Players work in pairs.
3. Partner A closes their eyes as Partner B leads them around the space.
4. Partner B's goal is to ensure their partner feels as safe as possible. They must determine what is best for their partner (without talking). It can be walking with both hands held, one hand held, an arm around shoulder, etc.
5. Let them wander for 2 minutes or so, keeping their movement slow at all times. Switch.

Reflection:

How did you make your partner feel safe? What did your partner do that made you feel safe?

Falling Backward (Trust Exercise #2)

Purpose: To elevate the comfort level and trust among the group.

Procedure:

1. This is the first activity of a falling series, so it may work best to demonstrate either with a brave student or with two teachers.
2. Working in pairs, Partner A stands with her back facing Partner B.
3. Partner A falls back (only a foot at most) into Partner B's hands.
4. Partner A shouldn't take their feet off the floor, allowing themselves to rock back on their heels only, and should just relax and breathe (may close eyes if they wish).
5. Partner B must assume a balanced stance (knees slightly bent, feet shoulder width apart and slightly staggered, hands up and ready to catch their partner).
6. Work until both partners are comfortable in both roles.
7. If players seem wary of safety because of weight differences, explain that they only fall a very short distance from their partner's arms and that this is an exercise more of balance than of weight.
8. Step in and help if you have noticeably uneven weight distribution between partners.
9. You can then rearrange players into groups of threes. One "falling" player stands in between the two "catchers" only on foot or so apart from each other.
10. The middle player can keep their arms down or cross them on their chest as they gently fall forward and gently pushed backward by the two outside students.
11. Remind the group that their job is to create a safe environment for their team.
12. Remind the "faller" to breathe and relax. Switch roles until all players have had a turn falling and catching.

Passed Around (Trust Exercise #3)

Purpose: To elevate the comfort level and trust among the group.

Procedure:

1. Players stand forming circles in small groups. (6-8 players in each group.)
2. One brave volunteer stands in the middle, arms crossed over chest.
3. When the player is ready, they may fall forward or backward and then be gently "passed" around the circle.
4. Keep the standing circle very tight so the falling player can be passed slowly.
5. Have all players be in a "ready balanced position" at all times.
6. Encourage everyone to have a turn falling. This is key for building a group that feels equally involved and responsible for one another.

Reflection:

What did it feel like to rely on someone else? To be responsible for someone else?

Exploring the Space

Purpose: To become familiar with the environment. Encourages kids to work together as a group.

Procedure:

1. Have players stand scattered all around the room.
2. Tell the group to start walking around the space.
3. As they walk, they should try to cover the entire space, making sure that they are evenly spaced across the room.
4. Players should be aware of each other but cannot speak or communicate in any way.
5. They most be in motion at all times and be careful not to touch anyone.
6. Tell them "Go".
7. Inform them you will instruct them to "Stop" at which point they must all freeze in place.
8. Have them get used to walking and stopping by calling out "Go" and "Stop"

There are many variations to this activity. You can play around with any of these variations that all encourage teamwork, awareness and communication:

- Players can cover the space in pairs or in threes.
- Have them vary their speed by calling out instructions to pace their walk at a 1 to 10, 10 being the fastest.
- At a stop, have players make different shapes with others using their body, for example one square or two triangles.
- Have players form groups based on the colors they are wearing, or the colors of their eyes, or the type of top they are wearing, or the type of music they listen to.
- These are all silent activities. It's interesting to see how players figure out how to arrange themselves in groups by their taste in music without talking to each other.

Do You Love Your Neighbor?

Purpose: To increase focus and decision making. Encourages the entire group to remain attentive at all times.

Procedure:

1. Arrange chairs forming a circle with one chair per player, minus one.
2. The extra player stands in the middle of the circle and approaches another player that is sitting and asks, "Do you love your neighbor?"
3. If that chosen player answers "Yes, I love my neighbor", the two players sitting on both sides of him quickly try to exchange seats before the middle player sits in one of vacant chairs.
4. If the chosen player answers "No," he continues the response with, "but, I love everyone who _____" (i.e. has brown eyes). Everyone in the circle with brown eyes must find a new chair before the middle player sits in one of the vacant chairs.
5. The player that does not find a chair to sit in becomes the new middle player standing in the center of the circle. Continue for several rounds until everyone has had a chance to ask, "Do you love your neighbor?".

Group Count (1 to 10)

Purpose: A useful game to play if you have teamwork, discipline or respect issues within a group. It's simple and focuses the entire group's energy on one simple task. When completed successfully the ensemble automatically feels a little stronger.

Procedure:

1. Group stands forming a circle and looks down at the floor.
2. Any player starts by saying "one."
3. Any other player continues saying "two" and so on until the group counts up and reaches "ten".
4. If any two players say a number at the same time the group must start over from the beginning at "one".

Group Shape

Purpose: To explore creatively as a group. Encourages communication skills.

Procedure:

1. The entire group stands in the space.
2. As you count down from 10 to 1, their goal is to create the shape of any object using their bodies (as a group).
3. When you reach "1" and say "freeze!" they must freeze as you inspect the group's object.
4. The first couple times don't provide any instructions and let them try to figure it out however they want, even if it includes talking. You'll notice a lot of personalities come out.
5. Then say they must work silently.

Variations:
- After awhile, consider dividing the class up into two or three groups. Call out an object and have them compete on who can create the best shape in 10 seconds. Then have each group create an object they picked, while the other groups have a chance to guess.
- Consider allowing only 5 seconds.
- Consider assigning an object that has motion and have them demonstrate the moving object.
- If you're rehearsing a play or musical, consider using objects/ themes found in the story.

Object Ideas:
- A plane
- An iPhone
- A piano
- A shoe
- A giraffe

- Fire
- A tree in a storm
- An eagle
- A blinking eye
- A ticking clock

Movement Objects:

Wizards, Giants, Goblins

Purpose: This is a creative version of "Rock, Paper, Scissors". Encourages physical movement and increases focus and decision making.

Procedure:

1. Divide the group into two teams. Each team starts on opposite sides of the "stage".
2. Each team quietly decides if they are going to be Wizards, Giants or Goblins.
3. The teams line up on either side of the stage facing each other.
4. You count 1, 2, 3. On each number the teams takes one step forward.
5. On "3" they become the character their team decided on:
   - Wizards – lean forward throwing their arms forward as if casting a spell and say "Shazzam"
   - Giants – put both hands above their head, stretching and standing up really tall and say "Ho, ho ho!"
   - Goblins – crouch down, put their hands up to their face as if scratching their beards and make a high pitch laugh.
6. Giants beat Wizards. Wizards beat Goblins. Goblins beat Giants.
7. The losing team must run back to their side of the room. The players on the winning team tries to "tag" as many of the losing team as possible before they're safe at home.
8. The captives now become part of their captors' team.
9. Continue until one team wins.

Give and Take

Purpose: To increase awareness of when to give focus and when to take focus. It's useful when beginning an improvisation unit, where you have a few kids who generally tend to dominate the scenes.

Procedure:

1. Divide the class into two groups.
2. The first group stands up and forms a semi-circle. The second group observes.
3. When you say, "action", there can only be one player moving (*taking*) at any given time. Everyone else must be frozen (*giving*).
4. Once another player starts *taking*, the current *taker* must stop and freeze (*give*). The *taker* must continue her movement until someone else begins to *take*.
5. The *taking* should pass randomly throughout the group. There should be no sounds.
6. There should be no overlapping *taking*.
7. Tell them that if you ever feel that the *taking* is being dominated by only a few players, or that too much overlapping is happening, you will say "Thank you" which means that group's turn is over and they all must sit down.
8. The second group stands up and forms a semi-circle. It's their turn.
9. Continue this exercise until you feel groups are working seamlessly and everyone is *taking* an equal amount. Make it a competition to see which group can stay up the longest.

Variation:

- Consider adding sounds in addition to movement.
- For advanced groups, consider allowing them to have one *sound taker* and one *physical taker* at any given time. (i.e. one person must always be making a sound and one person must always be physically moving)

Reflection:

- Was it difficult to wait your turn to *take*?
- How can this be useful when rehearsing a scene from a play?
- What skills were required to be successful as a group?

Toy Boat

Purpose: A simple trust exercise that encourages kids to work together and feel comfortable with the group. A useful game to play to calm the energy of a group.

Procedure:

1. The group stands forming a circle.
2. In the middle of the circle is a shallow pond.
3. Stand behind one player and ask her to close her eyes. As you gently push her forward, she is to become a *toy boat* that lightly glides to the other side of the pond (with her eyes closed).
4. When the boat reaches the other side, the player on the other side should be ready to catch her. The *toy boat* opens her eyes and takes the place of whichever player caught her.
5. The player who "caught her" now becomes the next *toy boat* to float across the circle.

Notes:

- Make sure that this game happens in a slow gentle motion.
- Players will realize when their eyes are closed the other side of the circle seems further than they think.
- After a few rounds, consider sending two or three toy boats across at the same time.

Balancing Plate

Purpose: This is a type of "mirroring" exercise with a whole new twist. Best for slightly older kids as younger kids may have difficulty grasping the concept.

Procedure:

1. The group forms a straight line across the stage. It must be an even number (if not, ask the extra student to be the "judge" for the game).
2. Have players count off starting from both ends. The two players at both ends are "1"s, the players next to them are "2"s, etc.
3. Make sure everyone knows their number partner by having them "wave" to their partner.
4. Place an object in between the two players in the center of the line (a chair, a bottle, etc.)
5. The group is standing on a giant "plate" that is being balanced on center fulcrum (or axis), represented by the object.
6. Each player and their partner may move anywhere in the space, independent of the other players, but must always mirror their partner's movements.
7. Additionally, both partners must stay the same distance away from the fulcrum or else the "plate" is off-balance and crashes. So, if Player 1 moves in close to the fulcrum, his partner must move in equally close. If Player 2 moves to one corner, far from the fulcrum, her partner must move the same distance to the opposite corner.
8. Start the game by calling out a number plus a leader, such as "1s Go! Josh, you're the leader!" Josh's partner (the other player 1) must then follow Josh's lead.
9. Gradually call on other numbers until everyone is playing.

Note: Consider using this activity as a way to introduce the class to the idea of "filling out" a stage picture or creating a balanced tableaux.

Towel Crossing

Purpose: Although this game isn't directly related to theatre or drama specifically, it's great for team building and encourages kids to think outside the box.

Materials: 1) A long beach towel 2) A hand towel (old ones that you don't mind getting dirty).

Procedure:

1. Divide the class into groups. Each group should have 4-8 students.
2. Clear the stage. With masking tape, create a starting line and finish line on opposite sides of the stage.
3. Ask one group to take the stage and line up behind the starting line. Give the group both the beach towel and the hand towel.
4. The goal of each group is to get from the starting line to the finish line as quickly as possible, while keeping everyone's feet ON the towels at all times.
5. If any team members' foot touches the floor, they must start over while the clock continues to run.
6. They can use any technique they can think of.
7. Use a stopwatch to time each team. The team that accomplishes this task the fastest wins.

Notes:

If the kids get stuck, coach players by asking, "How else could you use those towels to solve the problem?" or "Think outside the box!"

Minefield

Purpose: To increase proficiency using stage directions. (There's also a simpler version that can be played in the "note" below.)

Procedure:

1. Choose one player to be blindfolded.
2. Have players scatter the floor of the stage with random objects (a book, a crumpled piece of paper, a backpack, an eraser, etc.). These objects are the "mines".
3. Place the blindfolded player at one end of the stage, while the rest of the group sits in straight lines in facing the stage.
4. The goal is for the group to direct the blindfolded player from one end of the stage to the other without touching a mine, using precise "stage direction" commands. Each player gives the blindfolded player one direction.
5. For example:
   - 1st player: Take two small steps upstage.
   - 2nd player: Take 4 large steps stage right.
   - 3rd player: Take a tiny step upstage left. Etc.
6. If the blindfolded player touches a "mine", it "explodes" and their turn is over.
7. Choose another player to be blindfolded while the group rearranges the mines on stage and plays again.

Note: This game requires kids to already know the basics of stage directions. For younger kids, this game can be played using normal everyday commands as opposed to stage directions (i.e. "walk two steps forward").

Islands

Purpose: To increase awareness of physical space. Encourages kids to work together.

Procedure:

1. Place sheets of newspaper around the stage. They should not be touching and there should be enough space to walk around them. The number of sheets used should be one less than the amount of players.
2. The group is going on a swim in the ocean and the newspapers are tiny islands. The only problem is sometimes there are sharks in the ocean! Whenever you call out "Sharks!" each player must step onto the closest *island*.
3. You are allowed more than one person per sheet of paper.
4. A person is safe on the *island* as long as no part of their body is touching the surrounding floor.
5. After everyone is safely and completely on a sheet, call out "Swim" and the group can move around the room again.
6. Remove one or more sheets and repeat the process. End the game when the entire group has successfully placed themselves on the remaining pieces of newspaper. Or when they have collapsed trying!

Notes:

Consider using music for each new round of "swimming". Something tropical or Hawaiian might work well.

String Shapes

Purpose: To build teamwork and increase communication.

Materials: A long piece of string (or yarn, twine, rope).

Procedure:

1. Lay out a long piece of string in front of the class.
2. Have all players stand holding of a part of the string, holding it with both hands at waist level.
3. The goal is for the students to work together to create whatever shape you call out. The students must hold onto the string at all times and involve every student in the shape.
4. Begin with the simplest shape, a circle. Then a square, triangle, rectangle, etc. (For advanced groups; polygons, trapezoid, etc.)
5. Ask them to come up with some sort of gesture to signify they have completed the shape.
6. After they've gotten the hang of it, instruct them to make the shapes without speaking.

Variation:

• Consider asking the group to make two connected shapes (with the same string).
• Instead of shapes, consider asking them to create the outline of an object or animal.
• For advanced older students, consider challenging them to create a shape with their eyes closed. You may allow them to communicate with words for this challenge.

Affirmation

Purpose: Use this at either the very beginning or very end of a session (or rehearsal). If used at the beginning, it sets a positive and uplifting tone for the day's session. If used at the end, it will help kids feel good about what they've accomplished and leave feeling energized.

Procedure:

1. The group stands forming a circle while holding hands, eyes looking at the floor.
2. Going around the circle, each player says one word at a time, building upon one another to collectively create a phrase that sets a challenge for today's work (or positively reflecting on today's activity).
3. When the group collectively feels that the phrase is complete, they raise their hands in the air and step in the circle creating a big clump and shout, "Yes!".
4. The players then take their place back in the circle and a new phrase begins where they left off.

Example:

For the start of a session:
"Today...we...will...listen...and...work...together." ALL: "Yes!"

For the end of a session:
"I...learned...to...never...turn...my...back...to...the...audience." ALL: "Yes!"

Variations:

• Consider allowing the kids to come up with their own affirmative phrase instead of "Yes!"(i.e. Whoohoo! Totally! You got it dude! etc.)
• Instead of going in order around the circle, consider letting kids add words randomly in a "give and take".

People, Shelter, Storm

Purpose: To move as a group and increase focus. Increases decision making and attentiveness.

Procedure:

1. Clear a large space for players to move around.
2. Form small groups with three players each.
3. In each group, two players form a "shelter", while the third player is the person living in that shelter. A shelter is formed by two players facing each other, arms extended high with palms placed flat against each other to create a "roof". The person ("people") living in the shelter must duck underneath the shelter's arms.
4. You call out three possible words: "People", "Shelter" or "Storm".
5. When "People" is called out, the "people" must leave their "shelters" and run to a different one while the "shelters" stay in place. Practice this a few times.
6. When "Shelter" is called out, the two partners that form "shelters" must break apart and find a new partner to build a "shelter" over.
7. Practice this a few times, calling out the "People" command as well.
8. When "Storm" is called out, everyone runs around for 5 seconds, then new groups of 3 players should form using the 2 shelters and 1 person combination. During the "Storm", shelters can now become people and people can become shelters.
9. Continue the game, rotating callouts between "People", "Shelter" or "Storm".

Notes:

- If your group does not divide into threes perfectly, the teacher or assistant may have to play.
- For slightly older kids, consider letting a player be the "caller". When "storm" is called the "caller" joins the game and tries to find a group of 3. Whoever is left out becomes the new "caller".

Spy, Crush, Anger

Purpose: This game is similar to Enemy and Protector, but a slightly different take and a bit more involved. Encourages kids to observe and react using physical behavior.

Procedure:

1. Players silently walk around the space.
2. Instruct the group to pick someone in the space as "Target 1" to "spy" on. Players should continue to walk around as they silently spy on him.
3. Then instruct the group to pick a different person as "Target 2" to "spy" on. They must keep on eye on both targets while moving across the space silently.
4. After a while, instruct the group that they have a "crush" on Target 1" and must try to get as close as possible to that person, while continuing to "spy" on Target 2.
5. Finally, instruct the group that they are now "angry" at Target 2 and must try and get as far away as possible from her while attempting to remain close to their "crush", Target 1.
6. Observe the changing dynamics of the room.

Notes:

- Consider using this activity as a lead in for how physical interactions are affected by character motivations.
- How do you interact with someone you're friends with as opposed to someone you don't like very much? Why?

Index Card

Purpose: To break the ice. Encourages exploration and speaking in front of a group.

Procedure:

VARIATION 1:

1. Give every player a blank index card.
2. Every player must write down some thing that no one knows about them.
3. Collect, shuffle and randomly hand one card to each player.
4. The players must figure out who wrote the card, without directly asking "Did you write this?"
5. Afterword, have each player share with the group how they figured it out.

VARIATION 2:

1. Customize the prompt for players to write on their card.
2. You can have them write three things: favorite subject, favorite place they've ever visited, favorite song.
3. After each player finds the correct player who wrote the card, have each person introduce themselves and tell them a little bit more about their choices.

OTHER PROMPTS:

• favorite movie
• favorite time of day
• scariest nightmare
• favorite musical
• least favorite food
• favorite type of character to play
• favorite subject

A Fine, Fine Line

Purpose: To work creatively as a group. Encourages motivation and observation skills.

Procedure:

1. Have small groups with 6 to 8 players each.
2. One group takes the stage.
3. Instruct them to arrange themselves in a line according to specific criteria (for example; height order.) When they are finished they must call out "We're a fine, fine line, whoo!" (Or have them come up with their own silly phrase.)
4. Repeat the game with another group using a different criteria. Tell them to arrange themselves in a line according to:
   - age
   - shoe color (light to dark, dark to light)
   - shoe size
   - alphabetically (first name, middle name, last name)
   - hair color (light to dark, dark to light)

Variation:

- Let each group pick their own criteria. After they've formed their line, have the rest of the class guess what the criteria was.
- For older groups, consider assigning each group a "line leader". This "line leader" is the only person who can speak when organizing the group's line. She can ask questions to her group, but the players can only respond by nodding or shaking their heads.

BREAK OUT OF SHELL

Hot Spot

Purpose: To react quickly and identify patterns. Designed to get kids "out of their heads" and raise the comfort level of performing.

Procedure:

1. The group stands forming a circle.
2. One player steps into the center of the circle and starts singing a song, preferably one the group already knows.
3. After a few lines into the song a different player must step in and tap out the player in the center and take their place. That player then begins singing a new song inspired by the previous song.
4. That is the pattern, as player after player taps into the center of the circle to sing a song.
5. Players standing around in the circle may support the center player by singing along, clapping hands, miming instruments, etc.
6. Players standing around in the circle should be encouraged to provide support by tapping in, in order to move the exercise along and not leave the player in the center for too long.

Variations:

• Made-up Hot Spot: Like regular Hot Spot, except the songs are made up on the spot. Players in the circle are still encouraged to sing along.

• Monologue Hot Spot: The player in the center tells a story. Someone around the circle usually taps in before the story is over.

• Character Hot Spot: The player in the center tells a story as a character. The player may jump tap back into the circle at a later time, still acting as the original character.

• Misheard Lyrics Hot Spot: Songs are sung with lyrics that are close, but not quite right.

Conveyor Belt

Purpose: To be creative physically and respond quickly. Encourages kids to stay focused, memorize and juggle multiple steps.

Procedure:

1. Players stand in two equal lines facing each other just a few feet apart. Every player should be looking directly across from another player. (If space is tight make two sets of two lines.)
2. One line is "A" and the other line is "B".
3. When you call out "A", players in line A strike a pose, any pose each individual chooses. When you call out "B", players in line B mirror the pose of the player across from them.
4. When you call out "Shift", line A and line B shift one player over to their right. The players at the ends of the line, however, must cross over to the other line, from line A to B or B to A, and face the person in their old line. The line set up should be the same as before, where everyone is facing a partner, it's now just a new partner.
5. You will stand at the end of the lines and call out "A-B-Shift" over and over again.
6. You repeat the callout "A-B-Shift" until partners are back in their original position.
7. To make things fun, start off slow calling out, "A (one Mississippi, two Mississippi), B (ditto), Shift (ditto)" and then slowly speed it up so players are scrambling to keep up. (Note: If players get confused in where they are, point out that when they shift they won't end up facing the next player in line. They end up facing the player two players down. This will help in shifting.)
8. Now things really start to get fun. Repeat the process again, but this time players must strike a pose and make a noise.
9. For the final round, tell players to make a repeating motion and sound instead of a pose. Hopefully everything will break loose and players get outrageously ridiculous and giddy.

Sound and Motion

Purpose: To be responsive and creative. Encourages kids to make clear choices.

Procedure:

1. Everyone stands forming a circle.
2. The teacher starts by doing a simple sound and motion, which you will then pass to the player on the right to mimic, who passes it on to their right, and so forth around the circle.
3. Players should be ready to receive the sound and motion and immediately without thinking pass it on. Start with a simple and smallish sound and motion.
4. Continue until players respond automatically.
5. In the next round, instruct the group that they must make the sound a motion a little bigger each time its passed from player to player.
6. Continue until the sound and motion is huge.
7. As a possibility for the last round, instruct the group that they can alter the sound and motion as they make it bigger. Challenge them to challenge each other by getting more and more ridiculous. Each player topping the sound and motion of the player before them.

Other Variations:

Start sending one sound and motion around. Then, immediately send a new sound and motion going the opposite direction. Try to keep the ongoing flow of sound and motion going around.

Note: This game is simple and has many variations. It's recommended especially when working with image-conscious teens. Start simple and slow and work up to total craziness.

Enemy and Protector

Purpose: To focus and be aware of physical space. Encourages kids to react and remain attentive at all times.

Procedure:

1. The group stands scattered around the space.
2. Instruct the group to silently in their head pick a player in the room that will be their "Enemy".
3. Instruct the group to silently in their head pick a different player in the room that will be their "Protector".
4. Each individual player only knows their choices.
5. Once everyone has made their choices, you call out, "Go!" and everyone must try to keep the "Protector" between themselves and their "Enemy" at all times by moving around the room.
6. Ideally the group movement will work out in a way where everyone forms a line so that everyone has their protector between them and their enemy. However it is not the goal of the game and only rarely happens.

Ducks and Cows

Purpose: A fun way to split the class into two groups.

Procedure:

1. The group stands forming a circle and closes their eyes.
2. Go around the circle and tap players one by one.
3. A tap on the right shoulder makes them a duck. And a tap on the left shoulder makes them a cow.
4. When you say "Go" players open their eyes and must find the member of their duck and cow team by either "quacking" or "mooing".

Exaggeration Circle

Purpose: To make strong choices. Encourages even the shyest kids to be bold in front of a group.

Procedure:

1. The group stands forming a circle.
2. One player starts a small gesture.
3. The next player to the right takes it over and makes it even bigger.
4. This continues all the way around until the last person takes it to the EXTREME.
5. After a couple times with just movement, tell the players they can add a sound as well.

Note:

- Remind everyone to never lose a sense of the original gesture in their exaggerations.
- This can be a great lead in to character development, taking small traits and enhancing them to extremes.

Yes, No, Please, Banana

Purpose: To creatively perform a scene. Encourages kids to perform in front of a group and help break out of their shell.

Procedure:

1. Divide the group into pairs.
2. The goal of each pair is to create a 30 second scene using only four words: "Yes", "No", "Please" and "Banana".
3. Depending on the age group, encourage the players to include a range of emotions in the scene, and if possible to have a beginning, middle and end. Although many of the scenes will be silly, encourage them to try and make it believable.
4. Allow the group a few minutes to practice, then have them perform in front of the class.

Note:

Consider performing an example scene with an assistant before allowing the kids to create their own.

Deer!

Purpose: This game is similar to Bippity Bippity Bop, but is more physical. Encourages focus and quick decision making and teamwork.

Procedure:

PART 1
1. Divide players into groups of three.
2. Have each group pick an animal. Make sure there are no duplicates. Give the groups one minute to create a 3-person pose that represents their animal.
3. Gather the entire group in a circle.
4. Have each group teach everyone the pose that they created.
5. At the end review all the animals and poses. (You can write the list up on the board if it helps.)

PART 2
1. Choose one volunteer to be the leader in the center of the circle.
2. The leader points to a player and calls out an animal from the list, then quickly counts from 1 to 10. The chosen player and the players on both sides of her must create the animal pose before the leader reaches the count of "10".
3. If any of the three players fail to get into the pose in time, that player switches with the leader and calls out the next animal.
4. There is one catch. If the leader points to a player and calls out "Deer!", that player must freeze like a deer in headlights with eyes wide open. If the chosen player moves instead of posing like a deer, she must switch places with the leader.

Notes:

• The counting from 1 to 10 can happen very quickly. As the players get better, you can reduce the count to 5, and then 3.
• An alternative is to eliminate players instead of switching leaders.
• Why just animals? Feel free to experiment and have the kids create 3-person poses of anything within a theme.

FOCUS

Mirror Activity

Purpose: To increase awareness of body movement, behavior and teamwork.

Procedure:

1. Pair players up and let them pick who will be player A and B.
2. Inform A's that they are looking in the mirror. (Optional: Tell them it is morning and they are getting ready for the day.)
3. B's are the mirror image of A's and must mimic A so close that an observer cannot decipher who is leading and who is following.
4. Advise them to move VERY slowly.
5. Encourage them to mirror not only body movements but also facial expression.
6. Have them switch after a minute or so. Then announce that there is neither a leader nor follower. They should move as one. You may need to remind them to go very slow.
7. In the next round start with A's leading, but this time they are talking to themselves in the mirror as B's follow. Again let them switch and then try it with no leader and no follower.

Mirror Activity (4 Person Variation)

Purpose: To increase awareness of body movement and teamwork. It is best to play this after kids have done some mirror exercises.

Procedure:

1. Have four person groups stand facing their teammates. Assign numbers 1, 2, 3, 4 to players in each group.
2. As you call out a number, the specified player in each group is the leader and starts moving SLOWLY while the three other players in the group must follow the leader's movement.
3. The objective is for the four players to look as if they are moving as one, where an outsider cannot tell which player is the leader.
4. Give each "number" about one minute to be the leader, during which you can coach groups to move slowly and encourage them to remain aware of their movements.
5. Then open up a competition. Call out random numbers and switch it quickly. Meanwhile you and the other instructors can walk around the room and try to guess who the leaders are of each group.
6. Groups are tapped out when you correctly identify the player that is leading.
7. The last team standing wins.

Note:

Of course use your judgment when tapping out teams. Try to tap out teams that are clearly not in sync.

Who's The Leader

Purpose: To build teamwork and observation skills. Encourages kids to be aware of body movement.

Procedure:

1. One player leaves the room.
2. The remaining players stand in a circle and choose a secret leader.
3. The leader does a repetitive motion that the others follow. The leader will slowly change the motion while the others follow without missing a beat.
4. The player from outside returns to the room and attempts to figure out who is the leader.
5. He only gets two or three guesses.

Flock Dance (Variation of Mirror)

Purpose: To develop creativity, observation skills and group cooperation. Encourages kids to work as a team.

Procedure:

1. Players stand in a big group all facing the same direction (clump).
2. To start, a leader is chosen who is located in front of the group.
3. The leader slowly moves in a stylized walk or body movement.
4. All other players follow the leader.
5. If the group's direction changes, whoever is currently in the very front of the group becomes the new leader.
6. As with the mirror exercise, it should never be obvious who is leading the flock.
7. The exercise continues until several players have had the chance to lead the flock.

The Machine

Purpose: To develop creativity, concentration, and group cooperation.

Procedure:

1. The group stands in a circle formation.
2. Have one player start out by making a sound and a simple repetitive gesture.
3. When the first player has a rhythm down and another player has an idea for a movement that can connect with the first gesture, that player joins in. She makes a new sound and a new movement to connect with the first (as if to build a machine).
4. Every player will join in one by one with a new sound and gesture that connects until the entire group is involved in creating the machine.

Evaluation:

- What did you imagine the machine you created was?
- What was your part in making it?
- How could we make the machine batter?
- Was it difficult to keep your concentration until everyone was creating the machine?

Variation:

Decide on a type of machine and then have everyone create it together.

Rain Storm

Purpose: This is a helpful game to play at the beginning of a session to calm down a group of high-energy kids. It's simple, peaceful, and allows everyone to focus on one common goal.

Procedure:

1. The goal is to create the sound of a rainstorm using only your bodies. This requires no speaking
2. The group sits with you on the floor in a circle formation.
3. You (the leader) will start the action, then the player to your right joins in, the player to their right joins in etc. until the wave of motion reaches the full circle. Once it returns back to you (the leader) you start a different action which creates the second wave etc.
4. Players must carefully copy the movements of the player directly to their left and not switch actions until it is time to do so. Encourage the group not to focus on the leader, but instead only focus on the player to their left.
   • Action 1: Rub your hands together. (This is the wind)
   • Action 2: Tap one finger on the palm of your hand. (These are the first raindrops.)
   • Action 3: Tap all 4 fingers. (Many more rain drops.)
   • Action 4: Full on clapping. (It's getting more intense!)
   • Action 5: Slap on the floor, or your thighs. (Thunder enters!)
5. After the big crescendo, repeat all the actions in reverse order as the storm "dies down" — until you're rubbing hands together.
6. Then quietly stop. There should be absolutely silence.
7. Reflect on whether it accomplished the goal of sounding like a rainforest. Ask the players if there's any other activities they could add to make it sound more realistic? (Standing and stomping on your feet for thunder?) Ask what other environmental sounds could be created using just our bodies?
8. For an extended activity, divide players into smaller groups and give them five minutes to create their own "soundscape". Ask each group to share.

Twin Interview

Purpose: To build teamwork and listening skills.

Procedure:

1. Divide players into groups of three.
2. Each group selects one player to be the "interviewer" who asks questions, and the other two players will answer as "twins".
3. After the interviewer asks a question, the twins must answer in sync with each other, without discussing their answer between them. They have to listen to each other and speak at the same time with the same words in their response.
4. Give the groups a few minutes to practice.
5. Ask for a volunteer twin group to take "the stage". You and the class asks them questions one at a time.
6. Give several different volunteer twins a chance to take the stage.
7. Then move on with the same exercise, this time with groups of at least five, using the same principles. The group responds to questions as a single person with you or the rest of the group asking the questions.

Reflection:

Was this easy or hard to do? What made it easier? What skills were needed to make it a success?

Quick Change

Purpose: To hone in on observation skills. Encourages kids to take in and be aware of all the details around them.

Procedure:

1. The group is seated in a circle formation.
2. Pick one player to be the "changer".
3. She stands in the middle of the circle. The group studies her appearance for three seconds.
4. The "changer" leaves the room out of sight.
5. While outside the "changer" must alter three things about her appearance (pull a sock down, switch her watch from one wrist to the other, unbutton one button, etc.)
6. The "changer" returns.
7. The group must observe and figure out which three things were changed.
8. Continue for several rounds.

Sausage!

Purpose: To build focus and to stay in character. Encourages discipline and self-control.

Procedure:

1. Divide players into two groups, group A and group B.
2. Group A forms a single file line offstage right. Group B forms a single file line offstage left.
3. One player each, from group A and group B walks to the center. Player A faces Player B and ask him a question. No matter what the question is, Player B must keep a straight face and reply "Sausage".
4. They exit and a new pair takes the stage.

> EXAMPLE:
> A: What's that hanging from your ear?
> B: Sausage
> A: What's your sister's name?
> B: Sausage
> A: How old are you?
> B: Sausage.

5. Switch so that players in group A must reply "Sausage" to questions from players in group B.
6. After everyone has had a turn, select a few volunteers to go into the "hot seat". Ask several rapid fire questions, in which every response should be "Sausage" with a straight face. See if they can get through eight questions in a row without breaking.

Pass the Pulse

Purpose: A calm, silent game to help kids regain focus and work together. Helpful to play after a high-energy exercise, or at the beginning of a class if kids come in overly energized (commonly the case for afterschool programs!)

Procedure:

1. Everyone stands in a circle formation, holding hands with their eyes closed.
2. The instructor starts a pulse by lightly squeezing the hand of one of her neighbors.
3. Once that player feels the pulse, he squeezes the hand of his neighbor, and so on, until the pulse returns back to the instructor.
4. This should all happen silently.

Notes:

- If a player makes a sound or giggles, consider starting over again until the group can send the pulse around with complete control.
- For older players, consider sending two pulses around in same direction. Then send two pulses around in opposite directions.
- For a different experience, this game can be a competition. Have two lines face the other with the same amount of players each, with hands held, eyes closed and their heads bowed down. At one end of line is a chair with a tennis ball on it. At the beginning of the line is a "referee" with a quarter. The referee flips the coin and shows the result simultaneously to the two players at the front of the lines (they are allowed to have their eyes open). If the coin lands on heads, they must "pass the pulse" until it reaches the last person who must grab the tennis ball. The team that grabs the tennis ball first wins. If the coin lands on tails, no pulse should be sent.

Circle Switch

Purpose: To develop non-verbal communication and teamwork. Encourages camaraderie and quick decision making.

Procedure:

1. Players stand in a circle formation with one player in the middle
2. Two players along the circle discreetly cue one another to trade places.
3. The object of the game for players forming the circle is to switch places without attracting the attention of the player in the middle.
4. The goal of the middle player is to get to an open spot before the players that are switching make it to their new spot.
5. Whoever is left without a spot is now in the middle.

Rules:

• The players must move within the middle of the circle, not outside it.
• More than one pair can switch at a time.
• Players must not speak.

Reflection:

What sort of visual communication did you find works the best?

Silent and Serious

Purpose: To practice focus and self control.

Procedure:

1. Have players pair up.
2. Players stand back to back with their partner.
3. On the count of three, everyone must face their partner, while remaining silent and have a straight face.
4. Walk around as the inspector. The first person to smile or laugh must sit down.
5. Have the remaining players find new partners, then repeat the exercise again.
6. Keep going until there are only one or two pairs remaining.
7. If at the end no one breaks down, allow the rest of the group to act as hecklers to try and disrupt them.

Straight Face Introduction

Purpose: To be creative while remaining focused. Encourages self control.

Procedure:

1. Group stands in a circle formation.
2. Players must go around the circle one by one and introduce themselves. The catch is instead of using their real name, they must introduce themselves as the most disgusting food they can imagine.
3. Each introduction should follow this format: "Hi everyone, I'm [anchovy pizza with mustard on top], it's great to meet you."
4. The goal is for the player who is speaking to always keep a straight face, never laughing or breaking character. The rest of the group can, of course, laugh.

Variation:

Consider replacing [disgusting food] with any silly category you can think of.

For advanced kids, consider having them elaborate on their character for awhile. i.e. "Hi everyone, I'm pickled toenails with tartar sauce, my favorite hobbies are taking long walks, sunbathing, and chess. It's great to meet you."

CREATIVITY

Morph the Movement

Purpose: A good game for a medium or large sized group. A useful physical warm up with a focus on spontaneity and trusting your instincts.

Procedure:

1. Group stands in a circle formation.
2. The first player starts by choosing a physical action with repetitive motion (i.e. digging).
3. The player to his right imitates the action. So now two players are performing the identical action.
4. Once the first player feels that the second player has adopted the action to his satisfaction, he stops performing the action.
5. The second player now begins to loosen the action and exaggerate movement, morphing it until he has found a new action (i.e. throwing a ball). It should be noted that this is most effective when the transition is gradual. A result of a player listening to his own body as opposed to thinking of an alternate action.
6. Once the player to his right, the third player, feels that the second player has a clear action, he mimics the action.
7. The morphing of the movement continues until is has reached the end of the circle, at which point it can stop or go around again.

What Are You Doing?

Purpose: To develop focus and creativity. Reinforces the concept of having an activity vs. action.

Procedure:

1. There are eight volunteer players. Two standing in the front facing the audience and the remaining players line up behind them. There should be two rows of four people.
2. One of the two players in the front of the line starts an "activity" (brushing teeth, tap dancing, swimming).
3. The other player at the front of the line asks, "What are you doing?"
4. While player one continues to, for example, gesture brushing his teeth, he responds "I'm washing my car."
5. The second player, the one that asked the question must immediately gesture washing his car, while the first player goes to the back of the line and the next student moves up.
6. That player who just moved up immediately asks, "What are you doing?" Again the other player in the front must continue to gesture washing a car while he says, for example, "I'm curling my hair."
7. Continue until everyone has had a turn being in front.
8. Players are eliminated if they hesitate, freeze up or stop what they are doing. The question and answer pattern must be succinct. The correct response to "What are you doing?" should NOT match the player's gesture.
9. Continue until you are down to one player.
10. Bring up the next eight players and repeat.

Note: This could also be done in one big standing circle.

Group Environment

Purpose: To work on pantomiming and working as a group.

Procedure:

1. As a group pick an environment (i.e. kitchen).
2. One by one players enter the kitchen and mime interacting with one object, then exit. (i.e. a player enters and opens a refrigerator then leaves).
3. Each subsequent player that enters must use the objects that the players created before they entered. Each player must also introduce one new element. The next player to enter must remember everything that was used before him.
4. Emphasize the value of consistency of a physical environment. Did the sink stay in the same place every time? Did someone leave the refrigerator door open and the next player not think to close it?
5. Once the final player has completed his turn, reflect on the environment and have each player vocalize what object they created. You may be surprised to see how some things were not as clear as others.

Other Environment Ideas:

• Office
• Backyard
• Classroom
• Jungle

On the Spot

Purpose: To be spontaneous and stretch the imagination. Encourages kids to be creative as a group.

Procedure:

1. Players sit in a line facing the stage.
2. You announce a theme or topic.
3. Starting at one end of the line, each player takes a turn in standing up, walking on to the "stage" and striking a pose. The player should make a sound and/or motion that fits the theme.
4. For example, if the theme is "sports" one player stands, walks on stage, faces the audience and shouts, "You're out!", then exits the stage. A player could stand up and mime a basketball game, another could just be out of breathe and sweating.
5. Let every player go up. Then go down the line again with the same theme.
6. Keep it going even when it seems like there's nothing left to do. Keep pushing the players' imaginations. Anything is better than nothing.

Freeze and Justify

Purpose: To explore body movement and space. Encourages spontaneity, creativity and awareness of physical behavior.

Procedure:

1. Players walk around the space, constantly changing the movement and shape of their bodies, exploring unusual poses. Consider adding instrumental music to help their imagination.
2. The leader at any point calls out "Freeze!" at which point all the players freeze in their current pose.
3. The leader calls out a player's name and asks them to "Justify" their pose. For instance, a player posed with their arm raised high above their head might respond, "cleaning cobwebs from the ceiling" or "raising my hand in a classroom" or "playing basketball and just threw a three-pointer".
4. The player should imagine a situation in which their pose would make sense.
5. After the leader calls on three or four players to "Justify", unfreeze everyone and let them walk around again, posing and contorting some more. Repeat.

Stream of Consciousness

Purpose: To be spontaneous and make quick choices.

Procedure:

1. The group stands in a circle formation.
2. The Leader stands in center and gives one actor a word.
3. That actor must then just empty his/her head in a stream of consciousness that is evoked from that word. The actor must *never* stop talking.
4. The Leader will then pick up a word from that student and give it to the next actor to go on a stream of consciousness with.
5. Continue until everyone has had a chance.

Note:

- Encourage the kids to keep the flow going and never hesitate.
- Consider "eliminating" kids from the circle if they take too long of a pause.

Narrative, Emotion, Detail

Purpose: To make quick decisions and encourage creativity while following a format.

Procedure:

1. On three separate large cards write "N", "E" and "D". These stand for Narrative, Emotion and Detail.
2. Ask a player to take the stage and begin telling an improvised story.
3. Throughout the story, hold up either the "N", or "E" or "D" card.
4. If you hold up the "N" card, the player must add more *narration* or action to the story.
5. If you hold up the "E" the player must add more *emotion* to the story.
6. If you hold up the "D" the player must add more *detail* to the story (details about the environment, weather, colors, smell, sounds, etc.)

Variation:

- Consider having individual students in the audience hold up the cards. They should listen and be in charge of holding up their cards when they feel it's needed.
- Consider playing Conducted Story, but add the cards as an extra element.
- Consider keeping the cards around for any improvisation in which you want to challenge the actors to add more action, emotion or detail to their stories/scenes.

Environment Charades

Purpose: To create an environment while working as a group. Effective after kids are exposed to a significant amount of pantomime/space work (Group Environment, What Are You Doing?, etc.)

Procedure:

1. Divide players into groups of four or five.
2. Give each group a two syllable word. For this example, let's say "Carrot"
3. For each syllable, players imagine a "place" stemming from it. In this example players choose a garage (where cars are) and a garbage dump (where things rot).
4. For each place, the group of four decides who they all are and what they are doing in that space.
5. Groups rehearse their two scenes.
6. Each group performs their scene and the audience guesses the syllables and the word.

   Other Words that Work:

   • Nightmare
   • Seahorse
   • Pillow
   • Airplane

Note:

• The objective is for kids to use the environment. Doing activities that happen in that space. Let them know that relating to each other is not as important as interacting with the environment.
• This games is challenging and appropriate only for advanced kids.

Slow Motion Emotion

Purpose: To explore emotion, behavior and character work.

Procedure:

1. In a bowl, have slips of paper with different emotions written on them.
2. Three players come up on stage.
3. One of the players picks out a slip of paper from the bowl and shows the emotion written on it to the other two players.
4. Slowly count down from 10 to 1, while the players very gradually put that emotion in their bodies and their faces.
5. The audience guesses which emotion the players chose and reflect on what gave away that emotion.

List of emotions:

Friendly	Fascinated
Angry	Excited
Sad	Energetic
Embarrassed	Surprised
Frustrated	Grateful
Annoyed	Touched
Eager	Hopeful
Shy	Happy
Nervous	Peaceful
Loving	
Confident	
Proud	

Curious

Two Person Environment

Purpose: To be aware of physical environment. Encourages teamwork.

Procedure:

1. Group stands in a circle formation
2. Give players 30 seconds to silently in their heads pick a specific environment (i.e. the circus, a football game, detention, etc.).
3. Choose a player to start the game (Player 1). She steps into the circle and immediately acts within the environment she chose.
4. The player who was standing to her left (Player 2) in the circle joins the environment, once he becomes aware of what the environment is.
5. Player 2 says one line to Player 1.
6. Player 1 responds.
7. The scene is over and the pair take their place back in the circle.

Example:

Player 1 steps into the circle and immediately begins wiping sweat off her brow. Player 2 enters the circle and looks equally hot and exhausted, and tries to find some last drips of water from his canteen. Player 2 says "I don't know how you convinced me to go on this hike through the Sahara Desert." Player 1 says "Well, you said you wanted a vacation in the sun!" Scene is over.

8. Repeat in pairs going around the circle.

Bucket of Water

Purpose: To work on pantomime and to explore physical behavior and movement.

Procedure:

1. Two players take the stage. The rest of the group is seated in the audience.
2. The two players hold a large, imaginary bucket. One person is on either side.
3. The instructor fills the bucket with water from an imaginary hose.
4. The goal of the players is to carry the bucket from one side of the stage to the other.
5. Then they dump out the water and bring the bucket back.
6. The players should demonstrate the differences in weight of the bucket in their bodies and expressions.
7. Consider adding other elements to the activity: it's freezing cold, the bucket really smells, the floor is slippery, etc.

Beads on a String

Purpose: To be creative and make quick choices. Encourages teamwork.

Procedure:

1. Two players stand on opposite sides of the stage. Assign one player "A" and one of player "B".
2. Give both players 5 seconds to think of a random phrase.
3. Then ask "A" to share her phrase and immediately after ask "B" to share his phrase.
4. These two phrases are the first and final lines of a story.
5. One by one, the remaining group goes on stage and fills up the space between A and B (like beads on a string). Each comes up with sentences that fills in the middle of the story. (It's easiest to go in order from A to B)
6. After the "string" is completed, ask the whole group to repeat the story in order.
7. The challenge is to have the story make the most sense as possible.

Note: Most appropriate for older kids/teens.

Bus Stop

Purpose: To create a physical character through behavior and movement.

Procedure:

1. Have a bowl with slips of paper with different types of characters written on them (i.e. a 5-year old, a business person, a clown, an 80 year old, etc.)
2. Create a row of chairs (the bench) on stage.
3. Three at a time, players will enter the stage, sit and wait for the bus for awhile, then one at a time give up waiting and exit.
4. Before each player enters, they will draw a slip of paper from the bowl.
5. The objective is for the player to put that character into every part of their bodies and convey specific behaviors while in the scene.
6. After they exit the audience can guess the character of each actor.

Tour Guide

Purpose: To be aware of environment when creating a scene.

Procedure:

1. Pair players up.
2. Assign one partner "A" and the other partner "B".
3. Have everyone close their eyes and think of a physical place that is very special to them (playground, bedroom, kitchen, classroom, attic, Grandparents' house, etc.)
4. Coach them to picture their place in great detail. Imagine the colors, every object in the space, the lighting, the colors of the walls.
5. After a few moments, everyone opens their eyes.
6. Partner "A" should lead Partner "B" on a 2-minute guided tour of their special place, actually walking through the space you are in, but describing the physical details of their memory in specific detail.
7. Partner "B" can ask questions, and the guide may respond briefly. The focus should be on the tour itself.
8. After two minutes, switch roles and now Partner "B" will lead the tour.

Who's Telling the Truth?

Purpose: To work on conveying believable storytelling.

Procedure:

1. Divide groups into 3-4 players each.
2. Give all groups a topic, for example, "Your most embarrassing moment" or "A time you were really scared" or "Your favorite birthday party", etc.
3. Have players within the group share personal stories based on the topic.
4. Tell each group to choose one story they are going to tell.
5. Everyone in the group learns the story and tries to make it their own.
6. Each player in the group tells the story to the class and the class tries to guess who the story really belongs to.

Other topic ideas:

• Your best day at school
• Your worst day at school
• Your favorite trip you've taken
• The most famous person you've met

Two-Headed Monster

Purpose: To be creative and to encourage teamwork.

Procedure:

1. Ask two players to take the stage and link arms.
2. They are now a two-headed monster. As a two-headed monster, they talk in one-word turns, keeping the same personality.
3. Ask the group for a suggestion of an "object" or "place".
4. The monster must tell a story about that object or place, making it up as they go along.

Notes:

- Encourage kids to tell a story that has a beginning, middle and end.
- Coach kids to make a strong physical and character choice for their monster.
- The "two-headed monster" can be used within any other improvisation activity.

Variation:

- Instead of alternating word for word, players try to speak the same words at the same time.
- Consider trying a "three-headed" monster after the kids have become familiar with the activity.

Backdrop

Purpose: This game helps kids practice NOT being the center of attention. It's about creating an atmosphere, or backdrop, without taking focus. Encourages ensemble and teamwork.

Procedure:

1. Divide groups into 4-8 players each.
2. Each group must decide on an environment (i.e. the beach, a doctor's office, a playground, a bus stop, etc.)
3. The objective of the group is to create the scene's environment without any one person being the center of attention. They can use their bodies as props/objects within the scene, use sound effects, become secondary characters, etc.

Example:

Environment: New York City

- Player 1: A business person pacing around in the background, checking his/her watch constantly.
- Player 2: Standing tall with arms crossed to represent street signs.
- Player 3: A taxi driving through.
- Player 4: Offstage using her voice as a sound effect: "Honk!" "Honk!" "Hey outta my way!"
- Player 5: A tourist looking at a map, confused.
- Player 6: A broadway performer warming up his/her voice.

All of these things should be done subtly, never overpowering one another.

4. Give the groups a few minutes to practice, then call each group up to the stage one at a time.
5. When you say "action!" the background scene should come to life.
6. Ask the audience if it felt like a scene lacking a main character. If YES, the group accomplished their goal. Was anyone taking too much focus?

7. Allow the groups to adjust and try again until the balance is right.

Variation:

An alternative is to call this game "Extras". Every student in the background scene much be an actual character within the environment, but careful not to take focus once the director calls "Action!".

Don't Think

Purpose: Encourages kids follow their first impulses, to not think too much.

Materials: A stack of index cards. A hat, bowl or bag to place them in.

Procedure:

1. Hand out a blank index card to each player.
2. Have players write on open-ended or fill-in-the-blank phrase on the index card.

For example:
"My favorite time of day is _____."
"If I could be any superhero I would be _____."
"When I wake up in the morning, I like to _____."
etc.

(If your players are too young, consider creating all these phrases on your own ahead of time.)

3. Fold all the index cards in half and place them in the hat.
4. The group stands in a circle formation.
5. Pass the hat around quickly. Players must draw one card from the hat and answer it as quickly as possible, then pass the hat along. There are no wrong answers - just say whatever comes to your head first!
6. Begin the first round. Time them with a stopwatch.
7. Do two or three more rounds, each round they must beat their previous time. Encourage them to go faster and faster. Give them a goal, "Do you think you can do it within 60 seconds?"
8. By the 3rd or 4th round, they should be answering from their first impulse.

Reflection: What was it like to not think? Did you feel yourself censoring yourself in the beginning? What's the value of not censoring yourself?

Not What It Seems

Purpose: To think creatively and out-of-the-box.

Procedure:

1. On a small table place a variety of objects. The objects can be anything that the players can easily pick up (a paperclip, a fork, a plastic cup, a shoe, a comb, a book, an envelope, etc.)
2. Have players stand around the table.
3. Explain that the players are to go up one at a time, pick up an object and use it in a way that it's not normally used (i.e. a plastic cup becomes a tiny hat, or a fork becomes a comb, etc.).
4. For the first round players cannot use any words. Continue until everyone has had a chance. It's OK if an object is used twice, as long as it's not being used in the same way.
5. For the second round, have players say one line as they use the object.
6. For a third round (and for older players) consider allowing two players into the circle, each grab an object and begin a short scene.

Pop-Up Book

Purpose: An interactive way to have kids practice storytelling and body movement.

Procedure:

1. Ask five players to take the stage.
2. Assign one player to be the "reader". The other four players are the "pop-up book".
3. Ask the rest of the group for a suggestion for the title of the book.
4. Pop-up players lay on the ground, as if they are ink blots on the page.
5. Through pantomime, the reader opens the cover of the book and begins reading it. Whenever the reader flips a page, the four players "pop up" as if they were illustrations in the pop-up book. The reader must then "read" what is on the page, including the pop-ups into the evolving story.
6. Occasionally the reader can go up to one of the pop-ups and "pull a tab" and the character goes into a simple action. Or the narrator "presses a button" and a character speak a simple line of dialogue.
7. The objective is to create a story with a beginning, middle and end.

Notes:

- For each page turn, have the reader quickly move in front of the players with a big arm gesture as if turning a huge page.
- Encourage the pop-up players to use a range of positions and facial expressions.
- Remind the reader to use the frozen players as animate *or* inanimate objects...could be anything that helps move along the story.

Alternate Version 1:

If you have the time, consider beginning this game as a small 2 player activity to demonstrate how it works. One player as the reader, the other as a "pop up". Give the reader a simple title, such as "How The Monkey Became King" or "Tommy's Epic Day at School" or "Sarah's Magic Backpack", etc.

Alternate Version 2 (for very young kids):

A simple version of this game can be played by very young children. Simply have the children "pop up" as you, the teacher, narrates the story. This can be done as small groups or as a whole class. Remind the kids to stay very frozen after you flip the page.

Why Are You Late?!

Purpose: To work on pantomiming and communicating physically. Encourages teamwork.

Procedure:

1. Six players take the stage. Four players are "office workers". One player is the "boss". One player is the "late worker".
2. The "officer workers" sit facing the audience, miming typing on a computer.
3. The "boss" and "late worker" leave the room while the "office workers" come up with a reason why the "late worker" is late. (i.e. her hair got caught in the dishwasher!, her car got crushed by a dinosaur!, etc.)
4. Once the "office workers" have decided on a reason, they go back to typing at their computers.
5. The "boss" enters and stands with his back to the office workers so he can't see them. Then the "late worker" enters and faces the boss. The "late worker" can see the "officer workers", but the "boss" can't.
6. The "boss" asks the "late worker" So, why are you late?!
7. The "officer workers" stop typing and mime out the reason for lateness behind the "boss'" back and the "late worker" has to guess what it is.
8. At anytime, the "boss" can turn around to face the "office workers" – if he catches one of them not typing, that "officer worker" is fired and must leave the office.
9. The game ends when the "late worker" guesses the correct reason for lateness, or the "boss" fires all the "office workers".

Notes:
- The more silly the reason for lateness, the better!
- The number of "office workers" can vary.
- Consider limiting the number of times the boss can turn around if it becomes an issue.

Name Dance

Purpose: To individually explore movement and be comfortable in front of an audience.

Procedure:

1. The goal of this activity is for each player to create a dance piece that uses their entire body to spell our their name.
2. Start out by giving an example of a dance piece using your name.
3. Give the group two minutes to practice their dance pieces individually.
4. Have each player present their dance piece to the class.

Orchestra of Sound & Emotion

Procedure:

<u>VERSION 1: Traditional Orchestra</u>

1. Divide groups into 3 to 4 players each.
2. Groups sit in sections across the stage like an "orchestra".
3. Choose one player to be the "conductor".
4. The "conductor" stands in front of the stage and faces the "orchestra".
5. The conductor assigns each section an instrument (i.e. violins, trumpets, percussion, flutes, harp, cellos, etc). If necessary, explore what each of these instruments sound like.
6. One by one, the conductor points at each section to test out the instruments.
7. Then the conductor turns around, facing the audience and announces, "The next piece we will be playing is called [Swimming in December]" (She can make up any name he chooses).
8. The song begins. Each time the conductor gestures to a particular section, the performers make sounds of their instrument. When the conductor raises her hands high, the volume of the performers increases. Hands low, the volume decreases.
9. The song ends when the conductor raises her hands and quickly closes her fists.
10. The whole orchestra stands and takes a bow.

<u>VERSION 2: Orchestra of Emotion</u>

1. The setup is just the same as above, however instead of playing a specific instrument, the sections are playing a specific "emotion" (i.e. joy, fear, confusion, stress, anger, excitement, etc.).
2. The sections make sounds that reflect that emotion.
3. It's not necessary to have a title for each song in this version as it may confuse the emotions. Simply test out songs using different conductors.

Sound Ball

Purpose: To practice working with imaginary objects and devloping strong voices.

Procedure:

1. Everyone stands in a circle formation.
2. Explain to the group that in your pocket you have a very special, very magical sound ball.
3. Mime pulling a tiny ball out of your pocket and show it to the group.
4. It is a magic ball because the louder the sound you make, the bigger the ball grows. The quieter the sound you make, the ball shrinks.
5. Give an example of a loud sound, and mime the ball growing very large and very heavy requiring both hands to hold it.
6. Then give an example of a quiet sound, and mime the ball shrinking to something very tiny and light.
7. Pass this magic sound ball around the circle, and each player must make a sound to either grow or shrink the ball, then pass it to her neighbor. (If the kids are young they could just say their name.)
8. Remind the players that their whole bodies should reflect how heavy or light the ball is, especially when passing it the next player.
9. After the ball goes around the circle once, allow the players to pass the ball by bouncing it across the circle. Encourage them to make strong eye contract with whomever they are passing it to.
10. Once again, make sure the players keep track of how big or small the ball is.
11. At the end of the game, choose one player to be the "keeper" of the sound ball, and you will ask them for it the next time you play. Shrink the ball, hand it to the student, and have him put it in his pocket. The next time you play, they will ALWAYS remember who has the ball :)

Note: This activity can be used as a way to remind kids to use BIG voices on stage.

Famous People

Purpose: A game that involves the whole group. It can be tailored to reinforce characters in a specific play your class is studying or rehearsing.

Procedure:

1. Set up three chairs in front of a large writing surface (white board, chalk board, chart paper). The chairs face the audience, with the backs to the writing surface.
2. Ask three players to sit in the chairs.
3. On the board, behind each player's head, write down three famous celebrities. The audience should be able to see them, but not the players.
4. The goal is for the players to guess which celebrity they are by asking "yes" or "no" questions to the rest of the group. If they get a "yes" response, that player gets to keep asking questions. If it's a "no" response, the turn goes to the next player. Sample questions could be "Am I female?", "Am I a child?", "Do I get swept up in a tornado and land in Oz?", etc.
5. Continue until each player correctly names the famous person.

Notes:

- If you're rehearsing a specific play or musical, considering choosing only characters from the story.
- Instead of characters, you could also choose famous places.
- For younger groups, make the category as specific as possible.
- For older groups, consider creating a tournament situation where the first to guess correctly amongst the group of three is the "winner", and the "winners" will against each other in a final round at the end for the ultimate championship.

IMPROV

Emotion Party

Purpose: To explore emotions and be aware of surroundings.

Procedure:

1. Each player thinks of an emotion silently in their head.
2. One player (the host) starts in the center of the room, setting up for a party.
3. The host acts his emotion through his behavior and manner.
4. Another player knocks on the door and is let in by the host.
5. The new player must act in the manner of her own emotion.
6. The host, player one, now begins to act in the manner of the second player's emotion (having guessed what that emotion is).
7. A third player knocks and enters with a different emotion.
8. Now players one and two must independently identify the third player's emotion and begin to act in the manner of that emotion.
9. Game continues until all of the players have entered the party.
10. Players then leave the party, one by one, in the order in which they came in and with the emotion they chose.
11. This continues until the first player, the host, is all alone again, and is back behaving in the manner of his original emotion.

Notes:

- Try this activity first without any sounds, forcing the kids to think of how to demonstrate the emotion using only their bodies/expressions/actions.
- Consider adding speaking after doing it once without sound.
- Reflect on which way was most challenging, and why?
- Encourage the kids to always be aware of participating in believable activities with other members of the party.

Hitchhiker

Purpose: To work on quick decision making and creativity.

Procedure:

1. Place four chairs on stage to represent four seats in a car. Four players start in the car. They are headed somewhere.
2. A "hitchhiker" stands up and puts her thumb out. The hitchhiker has a very strong characteristic, such as enormous sneezes, extremely old in age, annoyed business person, etc.
3. One of the passengers says "look, hitchhiker" and they pull over to pick the hitchhiker up.
4. The hitchhiker enters the front passenger seat and the other players rotate around clockwise. The driver gets out of the car and exits.
5. As soon as the hitchhiker enters the car, all the passengers and driver immediately take on the hitchhiker's characteristics and to the extreme.
6. They continue dialogue until new hitchhiker shows up.
7. This round robin should move very quickly.

Note:

On the first day of a session, you can save the improvisation game for the last five or ten minutes to send them off with a bang.

The Expert

Purpose: A beginning improv exercise that encourages kids to quickly come up with original material.

Procedure:

1. Players are each "experts" on a particular subject.
2. Players take turns going in front of class.
3. You or the audience call out a subject that the chosen player is an expert in (i.e. cereal, hairstyling, fruit, Mexico, etc.)
4. The player must talk about that subject like an expert for one minute.
5. They should not stop talking and can say whatever comes to mind no matter how absurd. The only rule is they can never stop talking.

Note:

- Consider adding some sort of prop to make it more fun. Perhaps some silly professor glasses, or a clipboard, etc.
- With more advanced kids consider asking them to take on different personalities as well.
- For a more advanced version, see Talk Show Expert (following page)

Talk Show Expert

Purpose: To make quick and creative decisions.

Procedure:

1. Two players sit on chairs in front of the "audience".
2. One player is the "expert" and one is the talk show "host."
3. The host's job is to throw focus to the expert and the expert's job is to take focus.
4. The host can make up the name of their show and a silly song to introduce it.
5. The host asks the audience for an object and an action. This is what the expert will be an expert at.
6. For example, The host introduces: "Welcome to the _____ Show! Today we're here with Dan, who's an expert on teaching pigs how to do karate. Tell us more Dan..."
7. Dan has to go along with whatever the host has made up. (Remember, the expert knows everything and whatever they say, no matter how outrageous, it is always right.)
8. After the initial interview the host takes questions from the audience for the expert to answer. (This is a way for more players to participate, and students who are shy get to shine for a moment as they work their way up to being experts or hosts.)

3 Television Channels

Purpose: To explore physical improvisation and creativity.

Procedure:

1. Three players stand facing the audience.
2. The audience comes up with three television channels (soap opera, cartoon, sitcom, reality, etc).
3. One audience member has the remote control and calls out a particular channel.
4. The players must perform a scene from that channel.
5. When a new channel is called, actors must immediately transition into a scene on the new channel.
6. When a channel that was previously called is called again, actors must go back to exact position and moment from where they left off.

Status Exercise

Purpose: To explore different behaviors and character choices.

Procedure:

1. Explain and explore the idea of "status". We all have different status in different situations.
2. From now on describe it on a 1-10 scale: 10 being practically a god and 1 being the lowliest creature you can imagine.
3. What status are you? If a 10 walked in the room, would you talk to her? What about a 1?
4. When was a time in which you were a 10? In other words, when you had complete power and authority in a situation?
5. Have slips of paper each with a number from 1-10 written on it. Mix them up in a bowl or hat.
6. One at a time, players draw a number from a hat.
7. Without revealing their number, each player enters the stage, stands, and exits as that number.
8. The other players try and guess the number based on the behavior of the entrance and exit for the player that is up.
9. Player's can come up a few times until it becomes clear to the audience.
10. For more advanced groups, have two players take the stage and improvise a scene (you can give them a setting and conflict if needed). Assign one player a "high" status and the other a "low" status.
11. Halfway through, tell them to "switch" statuses. Make sure they don't switch characters, but only who is in control of the situation, keeping their original characters.

Reflection:

- Explain that status is one more layer they can add to their characters.
- If you are rehearsing a play, ask them to think about each scene their character is in and what "status number" their character would be. What factors are influencing their level of status?

Grab a Slip

Purpose: To be creative and make bold decisions and responsiveness.

Procedure:

1. Create slips of paper with random phrases on them. (i.e. "The goats left for dinner already", "Never point at a pine tree", "Please stop looking at my earlobe", etc.)
2. Spread the slips of paper face down on the floor of the stage area.
3. Ask two or three players to start an improvised scene.
4. During the improv at random intervals yell, "Grab a slip!" The player that was speaking must bend down in mid-sentence and grab a slip of paper, say the line, and somehow justify the line within the scene.

Note:

- Encourage all the actors to do the best they can to stay in character and allow the line to become part of the scene.

<u>Other Random Phrases:</u>

- "Dominoes aren't meant to be left in the sun."
- "Explain yourself, quickly!"
- "My mouth feels like wet velcro."
- "Never underestimate the importance of clean underwear."
- "One time I tried to jump over a peach tree."
- "You look like a confused dinosaur."
- "Let me brush that for you"
- "Does my voice sound like a tiny robot?"
- "If only everyone could see me now!"
- "I think I'll go to sleep on that squirrel."

Gibberish Interpreter

Purpose: To be creative and make bold decisions.

Procedure:

1. If you haven't already, introduce your students to the idea of speaking in "Gibberish". (Gibberish means speaking with silly sounds that don't mean anything, but still communicate an intention and meaning.)
2. A good way to warm up the group is with a simple call and response. Speak a phrase in gibberish, and have the players repeat it. Try to use gestures and demonstrate different emotions and styles.
3. Then have two players take the stage.
4. One player speaks gibberish and the other translates the gibberish into English.
5. Give the gibberish speaking player a specific situation to talk about, or take suggestions from the class. (i.e. You have just come back from a walk on Jupiter, and you are telling us, a crowd of reporters, all about it.)
6. The gibberish speaker should speak only one line at a time, using as much physicality as she can. Then the interpreter must mimic the motions and translate the phrase into English.

Note: Encourage the gibberish speaker to be very specific in her intention and actions. Encourage the interpreter to think very carefully about trying to make the gibberish make sense.

Other Scenarios:
- A scientist explaining her recent discovery of a second moon
- A pop singer giving a press conference after falling asleep during his concert performance
- A child describing what it was like getting her first cavity
- A chef explaining how to cook his favorite meal, candy spaghetti (or anything else!)
- A farmer explaining how to milk a cow in record time

Gibberish Conversation

Purpose: To be creative and make bold decisions.

Procedure:

1. Before playing this game, introduce Gibberish to your students with a game like Gibberish Interpreter.
2. Two players take the stage as performers in the scene.
3. Two other players stand on either side of them. They are the interpreters.
4. Give the main players a topic. (Or ask for a suggestion from the class.)
5. The first player speaks a line in gibberish, then his interpreter will translate it into English for the audience.
6. The second player responds in gibberish, then her interpreter translates.

For example:

Topic: Laundry

Actor 1: Gil frelic neber seber trolli?
Interpreter 1: Is that pleasant smell coming from you?
Actor 2: Poy yoy, beek ploter woter magory.
Interpreter 2: Why yes, last night I washed my clothes in my dad's cologne.

Alphabet Conversation

Purpose: To make quick decisions and work as a team.

Procedure:

1. Two players take the stage.
2. Pick a letter from the alphabet to start with.
3. They must exchange dialogue in which the first word they speak must begin with the next letter of the alphabet, starting with whichever letter is elected and finish at the letter just before.
4. The conversation should make sense and propel action in the scene.
5. It's optional to give the players a given situation or scene beforehand.

<u>For example:</u>

"Fishing in the middle of a Lake", starting letter is "D".

Player 1: Do you want to add more bait to your hook?
Player 2: Eel or should I use squid?
Player 1: Forget eel, squid is the way to get the really big fish!
Player 2: Gonna give it a shot, here I go!
Player 1: Holy cow, nice cast!
Player 2: I've been practicing all summer...*etc.*

Yes, Let's

Purpose: This game reinforces the basic principle of improv – accepting. Kids are often contrary in their choices when starting improv. Because it's easy and often gets a laugh from their friends. However being contrary, or blocking, is fatal to most improv activities.

Procedure:

1. Divide everyone into two groups.
2. Ask the first group to take the "stage".
3. One player in the group starts by saying "Let's [____]" and then an activity (i.e. "Let's go to the mall!", "Let's do our homework", "Let's go surfing" etc.)
4. Then all the other players on stage support the action by jumping in and saying "Yes! Let's!"
5. Everyone then proceeds to do the activity together until another person in the group introduces a new "Let's [activity]!"
6. Everyone else says "Yes! Let's!" and proceeds to do the activity. (Encourage the players to always be physically active.)
7. This pattern continues until everyone has had a chance to suggest an activity.
8. After the first group finishes, ask the second group to take the stage and do the same.

Reflection:

- Was this activity difficult or hard?
- Did it make things easier/smoother knowing that you HAD to accept the activity?
- Did you feel more connected with your group by the end of the activity?
- How would this activity be different if you were allowed to "block" the suggestion?

Stand, Sit, Bend

Purpose: To work on physical improvisation and increase attentiveness. Encourages teamwork and focus.

Procedure:

1. Three players take the stage.
2. Ask one player to stand, one player to sit in the chair, and one player to bend over.
3. They improvise a scene (from an audience or teacher suggestion) where at any given point there must be someone standing, sitting and bending. (Example Scene: Two students who are being disciplined after school by their teacher.)
4. If any one player changes their position during the scene, the other two must compensate.
5. As the players get better at this game, encourage them to justify their positions as they change throughout the scene.

Variation:

If at any moment two players are in the same position consider ringing a bell to help warn them (or give this job to a student in the audience). They must immediately adjust.

Note: This game is best for older/advanced kids.

A Night at the Oscars

Purpose: To be creative and get out of your heads. Encourages teamwork and improv skills.

Procedure:

1. On stage create three groups of two players each, plus one "host". Everyone else should sit in the audience.
2. Have the audience suggest three fictitious titles for movies and assign them to each of the three groups. ("Planet of the Apricots!", "A taco paradise", etc.)
3. The activity then plays out like a night at the Oscars, with the host presenting.
4. The host one at a time introduces the movies, and the groups come up and present their Oscar-winning scene.
5. At the end, the host has the audience vote on the winning scene.
6. The winning group comes forward and gives an improvised acceptance speech.

Superheroes

Purpose: To be creative and get out of your heads. Encourages teamwork and improv skills.

Procedure:

1. One player takes the center stage. Three other players line up offstage.
2. Get an audience suggestion for a made-up superhero (Laundry Man!, Captain Toothbrush!, The Invisible Pancake!, Princess Talk Too Fast!, Dr. Never Smile! etc.) The player onstage takes on the identity of the selected character.
3. Now get an audience suggestion for a crisis (An asteroid is headed toward earth!, The Internet is down!, You've run out of milk!). The crisis can be large or small.
4. The player onstage, as the superhero, starts the scene with a monologue, explaining the crisis. (To propel the scene, consider having her turn on the radio or TV to discover the problem.)
5. When the first player says, "If only I had some help!" a second player enters. The first player endows the second player with a superhero name. ("Thank goodness you're here, Wink Girl!"). The second player takes on that character and joins the scene.
6. After a while of attempting to solve the crisis, a third player enters and the second player endows him with a superhero name.
7. Finally the fourth player enters and the third player endows her with a superhero name.
8. The scene continues until the superheroes find a reason to exit, in opposite order that they arrived.

Scene from Real Life

Purpose: To translate ideas and convey them to others. Builds directing and communication skills.

Procedure:

1. Divide groups with 3 to 4 players in each.
2. One player in the group must tell the others a true story about an event in her life. Encourage her to describe it in as much detail as possible. This player is the "director".
3. The director then chooses players of the group to play the various characters involved in the scene (including herself).
4. The players improvise the scene in front of the director.
5. After each run through, the director should give notes. Then the group improvises the scene again. The goal of the director is to make the scene as believable as possible. (Because the director is vividly familiar with the real life event, it becomes easier to give notes and adjustments. The skill being developed is the ability to effectively communicate these ideas to actors.)
6. Once the directors of each group are satisfied with their scenes, have the groups share in front of each other.

The Coffee House

Purpose: An improvisation game for more advanced kids. Incorporates elements of improv, gibberish, sound and movement.

Procedure:

1. The room is transformed into a bohemian coffee house. The stage becomes a small performance area within the coffee house.
2. Ask 4 players to take the stage.
3. Assign each player a role as follows:

- Player 1 = Foreign Poet (he/she must choose a specific country to be from)
- Player 2 = Musician
- Player 3 = Interpretive Dancer
- Player 4 = Translator

4. The players present a poem to the coffee house audience. Ask the audience for a suggested title for the poem.
5. Once the title has been decided, the Foreign Poet presents first. The Foreign Poet improvises a poem from the suggested title using gibberish that resembles the country he/she is from (length should be about 4 stanzas).
6. Next, the Musician provides musical accompaniment for the Interpretive Dancer who translates the poem into movement.
7. Finally, the Translator translates the poem into English for the audience.
8. Encourage the Musician, Dancer, and Translator to mirror the same emotion of the Foreign Poet when presenting their interpretations.

Notes:

- Consider encouraging the foreign translator to include rhymes into the poem (in gibberish). This will help give it a sense of rhythm.
- If you have a big class and would like to involve more students, consider doubling up on the Musicians and Dancers.

Fast Forward/Rewind (DVR)

Purpose: To work on physical improvisation. Encourages kids to get out of their heads.

Procedure:

1. Two players take the stage to create a scene.
2. Ask the audience for a suggestion of a "who" and "what" (Who the players are and what are they doing.)
3. A third player is the "Remote Holder".
4. The scene begins.
5. At any moment in the scene the "Remote Holder" can call out commands like "Pause", "Rewind", "Fast-forward", "Slow Motion", and the players must act accordingly.
6. After a while allow a new set of players take the stage and start the process over again.
7. Some ideas for the "Remote Holder" include using the commands to make a player say a funny phrase of dialogue over and over again, or "pause" in a silly way, etc.

Note:

- If trying to include more kids, consider having three players improv a scene instead of two.
- Consider giving the "Remote Holder" a character like "Lazy dude on couch" or "Hyper 8-year old". The player must act as this character when calling out the different commands.

Split Screen

Purpose: To focus and work on attentiveness. Encourages teamwork and creativity.

1. Split the stage into two halves (a split screen). Ask two players to take the stage on the left half, and two players to take the stage on the right half.
2. Ask the audience for a suggestion for a setting for each half. (i.e. left side is a *circus*, right side is a *dentist's office*.)
3. The players on the stage right half begin a scene while the other half remains frozen. When there is a word or phrase that the players on the stage left half could use as a beginning to their scene, they repeat that word and begin their scene from that point. When this happens the stage right players freeze.
4. The two halves continue on with their scenes, each freezing when the other half is performing.
5. The goal for each half is to somehow find a way to bring the scenes together (i.e. A circus performer chips a tooth juggling and must be rushed to the dentist! Or the dentist becomes completely bored with his job and decides to join the circus!)
6. When the two halves come together, the "divider" disappears and all four players briefly continue their scene until the instructor ends the game.

Note: This game is most appropriate for advanced students.

Fortunately, Unfortunately

Purpose: Similar to one word story, this is a beginning improvisation game that helps kids create interesting stories by thinking quickly and creatively.

Procedure:

1. Players stand in a circle formation.
2. The objective of the group is to tell a coherent story going around the circle. Each player contributes one line at a time.
3. A leader will begin the story with one establishing sentence.
4. Then every line must alternate between beginning with "Fortunately..." and "Unfortunately...".

Example:

- Leader: "Once there was a monkey who wanted to be a movie star."
- Player 1: "Unfortunately, she lived in the wild far away from civilization."
- Player 2: "Fortunately, she had a cousin who lived in Los Angeles."
- Player 3: "Unfortunately, she had no money to buy a plane ticket to Los Angeles."
- Player 4: "Fortunately, she was a very fast at swinging through trees so she began her journey to California."
- Player 5: "Unfortunately, her arms go so tired she had to stop and take a nap in a bear cave."
- Player 6: "Fortunately, the bear was out running errands so she had the whole cave to herself."

Helping Hands

Purpose: A classic game that encourages creativity, quick thinking, and requires excellent focus. Most appropriate for slightly older kids.

Procedure:

1. Four players take the stage, two on each side.
2. For each duo, one will be the "voice" and the other will be the "arms". The "voice" player stands with his hands held behind his back while the "arms" player stands behind him, pokes his hands through and provides the "arms".
3. Give the players a 2-person scenario (see list below).
4. The goal is for the players to act out the scene, having the arms and voice match and seem like one character.

Sample Scenarios:

• A principal lecturing a student for bringing his pet monkey to school.
• A chef teaching a student how to make pizza, but the student keeps eating the ingredients.
• Two muscle-builders at the gym who keeps trying to out-do each other.
• A grocery clerk and a customer checking out. The grocery clerk keeps falling asleep.

Notes:

• Encourage the "voice" players to try and justify all the movements made by the "arms".
• Encourage the "arms" players to listen carefully to the "voice" while from time to time making physical liberties of their own.
• Encourage all players to take their time and try to remain in character.
• This game can also be used as a variation of The Expert, in which the Expert is played by a "voice" and "arms" player.

Slide Show

Purpose: To make quick decisions and work on pantomime. Encourages teamwork and collaboration.

Procedure:

1. 6 players take the stage.
2. Players 1 and 2 are a couple (or friends) who recently went on vacation. They are showing the audience a photo slide show of their vacation.
3. Players 3, 4, 5 create the slides with their bodies through pantomime.
4. Player 6 is the "clicker", who dims the lights between each slide.
5. Each time the "clicker" dims the lights, Players 3, 4, 5 create a different pose.
6. Then the "couple" explains which part of their vacation is shown and exactly what is happening in the photo, justifying the players poses.

Notes:

• Consider asking the audience for a suggestion of where the vacation took place before beginning.
• Consider adding fun comments like "Oh, looks like that slide is upside down!".

Relationship Blitz

Purpose: A fast-paced improv game to help kids quickly establish relationships. Involves the whole group. Best for slightly older students.

Procedure:

1. Group stands forming a circle.
2. One player stands in the center.
3. Tell everyone in the circle they have 15 seconds to think of a specific relationship and situation they have with the person standing in the center (i.e. a robber breaking into his house, a young sibling asking for help with homework, a parent reading his terrible report card, a stranger asking for directions, etc.)
4. One by one, each player steps into the center and interacts with the center player with one line of dialogue. The center player, without being told the relationship, must respond with one line as quick as he can.
5. The game ends when everyone around the circle has had a chance to interact with the center player.

Note: To start, you may need to take it slow, but as the kids get better encourage them to speed up the pace.

Variation:

For more advanced students: After a few rounds, allow the greeting to turn into mini scenes. Then when the next player steps into the circle, challenge the students to make the scenes build upon each other to build a narrative.

Join the Beat by Beat Community

Sign-up at the address below to receive
FREE weekly updates with new drama activities:

www.bbbpress.com/dramagamesbook

Join over 9,000 subscribers!

Made in the USA
Monee, IL
15 September 2020

42488637R00075